the
receivers

Published by Creative Educational Society, Inc., 123 South Broad Street,
Mankato, Minnesota 56001. Copyright© 1975 by Creative Educational
Society, Inc. International copyrights reserved in all countries.
No part of this book may be reproduced in any form without written permission
from the publisher. Printed in the United States. Distributed by
Childrens Press, 1224 West Van Buren Street, Chicago, Illinois 60607
Library of Congress Numbers: 74-23400   ISBN 0-87191-418-2
Library of Congress Cataloging in Publication Data
Smith, Jay H.   The receivers.
(Stars of the NFL)
SUMMARY: Brief descriptions of the football careers of Charley Taylor,
Fred Biletnikoff, John Gilliam, Otis Taylor, and Paul Warfield.
1. Football—Biography—Juvenile literature.   2. Passing (Football)—Juvenile literature.
3. National Football League—Juvenile lit.
[1. Football—Biography.   2. Passing (Football)   3. National Football League.]
I. Biever, Vernon J., ill   II. Biever, John, ill.   III. Title.
GV939.A1S63   796.33'2'0922   [B] [920]   74-23400   ISBN 0-87191-418-2

stars
of the
NFL

the
receivers

by Jay H. Smith
photos
Vernon J. Biever/
John E. Biever

CREATIVE EDUCATION, MANKATO, MINNESOTA

the receivers

John Gilliam

22

Otis Taylor

32

Paul Warfield

40

Early in the 1971 season the Washington Redskins were setting the National Football League on fire. Undefeated through the first 5 games, they seemed on the verge of making it 6 in a row over the Kansas City Chiefs.

Washington had built up a 17-6 first-half lead, the result of the heroics of wide receiver Charley Taylor. In less than 30 minutes of football, Charley had made a shambles of a fine Kansas City defense. His 7 pass receptions had accounted for 125 important yards. Twice he had broken away to score.

On the second Redskin touchdown, Charley was tackled just as he crossed the goal line. The Chief defender released his hold, but Charley couldn't get up. He lay there on the green turf in terrible pain. The blow had broken Charley's ankle. He would be sidelined for the rest of the season.

The second half of the Kansas City game was a preview of just how much the Redskins would miss Charley Taylor. With Charley out of action, Washington's passing attack crumbled.

The Chiefs roared back to win, 27-20. Adding to the Redskins' frustration was the bitter fact that the winning touchdown had come on a daring one-handed catch by a receiver named Taylor. But he was the great Otis Taylor of the Chiefs.

From then on, Washington never managed to get rolling again. Finishing the year with a 9-4-1 record, the team had played average ball without Charley.

Because of their early-season edge, however, the Redskins still qualified for

Charley Taylor

the play-offs. But things continued to go from bad to worse, and Washington was knocked out of contention in the play-off opener.

In 1972, Charley Taylor came back for his ninth NFL season. This time he avoided injury, and the Redskins reached the play-offs once again. Washington defeated Green Bay in the first play-off game. Then they prepared to take on the Dallas Cowboys for the conference championship.

To his teammates, Charley is not only an exceptional receiver, but as one of Washington's captains he is a respected leader.

Before the Dallas game, he worked with Coach George Allen to make sure the team would be emotionally ready to play. Charley wanted to convince the Redskins that they could beat the defending Super Bowl champions.

And convince them he did. Washington dominated every aspect of the game and crushed the Cowboys, 26-3. The victory meant that the Redskins would go on to play the unbeaten Miami Dolphins in Super Bowl VII. For Dallas, victors in Super Bowl VI, the season had come to a gloomy end.

The Cowboy game was one of the finest of Charley's remarkable career. In the second quarter, Washington held a slim 3-0 lead. Then Charley went to work. After cleverly sidestepping a linebacker who had tried to cut him down, Charley headed down the sideline.

Only cornerback Charlie Waters was there to defend against him. Proving how difficult he is to stop in a one-on-one situation, the Redskin receiver raced by Waters. Quarterback Billy Kilmer floated the ball into Charley's hands for a 51-yard gain to the Dallas 21-yard line. Three plays later Charley fooled Waters again, this time going 15 yards for the touchdown.

Later, Charley did it again. Dancing past Mark Washington, who had replaced Waters, Charley sped to a second touchdown. The play covered 45 yards. All in

all, he caught 7 passes for 146 yards that memorable afternoon.

After the game Charley said, "People were saying that I had lost my speed because I broke my ankle last year, but I don't think I have."

Charlie Waters had to agree. "I had Taylor well covered," the Dallas cornerback remarked unhappily, "but he just ran away from me."

On January 14, 1973, Charley's dream of a victory in Super Bowl VII came to an end. The Miami Dolphins completed a perfect season with a convincing win over the Redskins. Charley never got much of a chance to show how effective he can be. All the game he was double-teamed, with 2 Miami defenders covering him closely.

Although his team had not won the Super Bowl, it had been a big year for Charley. Because of his impressive performance throughout the 1972 season, he was picked to play in the

10 Pro Bowl game. Charley had made the Pro Bowl squad all of his first 4 seasons in the league. Then he had not been selected for the next 4. After such a long absence, Charley was glad to be back in the limelight.

And he remained there. Following the 1973 season, his tenth in the NFL, Charley made his sixth appearance in the Pro Bowl.

Charles R. Taylor was born on September 28, 1941, at Grand Prairie, Texas. Following an outstanding college career at Arizona State University, he joined the Redskins in 1964. An immediate success as a running back, Charley was voted NFL Rookie of the Year.

Two years later, however, Otto Graham became head coach of the Redskins and converted Charley to wide receiver. At first Charley was upset by Graham's decision. "I felt I was getting my momentum going as a running back. All of a sudden Coach Graham

switched me, and I wasn't very happy about the change," he later told a reporter. "But the coach said he thought I could help the team more as a split end, and I think that's what kept me out there."

He was also a little afraid of making the move. Charley had never had very much experience as a receiver, even in college. "I did catch the ball quite a bit as a running back my first 2 years in the NFL," he once remarked, "but I never thought I had the ability to go out and maneuver a back one-on-one."

Charley admitted that he was rather frightened of the speed of the top NFL cornerbacks. He considered them much faster than he was, and that bothered Charley.

He soon learned that he could do something about the problem. Because he reacted so quickly, Charley discovered that he could outsmart most defensive backs. "I try to get right up to a guy," he has said, "and then move away in a hurry from him, and that's enabled me to get open."

In 1966, his first year as a receiver, Charley led the NFL with 72 catches for over 1,100 yards. Twelve of his receptions produced touchdowns. The following year Charley finished on top again, this time with 70 catches and 9 touchdowns. In both campaigns he was selected All-Pro. In a very short time, Charley had become a great receiver. He would remain so for many years.

Although Charley always denied that he has blazing speed, many of his opponents over the years strongly disagree. Yet they all know that Charley Taylor's greatness depends upon more than the quickness of his feet.

Throughout his 10-year pro career, he has worked hard to master the art of running pass patterns. As football has become more sophisticated, Charley has developed right along with it.

Unlike many wide receivers, Charley is an efficient blocker. At 6-feet-3-inches and 210 pounds, he always had the size and strength for the job. But, as with all things in his pro football career, Charley spent long hours learning how to do it well.

Charley's hard work has benefited more than one Washington Redskin ball carrier. Teammate Larry Brown has said, "There's no doubt in my mind that he's the best blocking receiver in football."

Although Charley does so many things well, he is not without weaknesses as a player. Some NFL defensive backs feel that he can be rattled and forced to lose his concentration at times. Recognizing this, Charley has had some success in correcting the problem.

Such devotion to excellence truly marks Charley as a pro among pros.

The air was charged with excitement as the Oakland Raiders opened training camp in the summer of 1965. Oakland's coaches were eager to find out what their rookies could do now that they were pros. One new player who really interested them was a young wide receiver named Fred Biletnikoff.

At Florida State University Fred had earned a solid reputation as a pass catcher. In his senior year he had been named to numerous All-American teams. The highlight of his college days had come against a powerful Oklahoma team in the Gator Bowl game. Fred had been sensational that day, catching 4 touchdown passes in Florida State's 36-19 upset victory.

The Raiders had every reason to expect a great deal from him. But during the first workout, the Oakland coaches took one look at the way Fred was running and simply couldn't believe their eyes. He was so slow that they thought he would never be able to make it in pro football.

Scouting reports on Fred had indicated that he wasn't very fast, but the Raider staff had not expected anything like this. They were keenly disappointed.

Fred's lack of speed wasn't his only problem during training camp that year. Playing against veteran pros made the rookie extremely nervous.

He always felt intense pressure whenever the ball was thrown to him. Then he would try too hard, and easy passes would bounce off his fingertips. Whenever that happened, Fred was sure he would be cut from the team.

Fred Biletnikoff

16

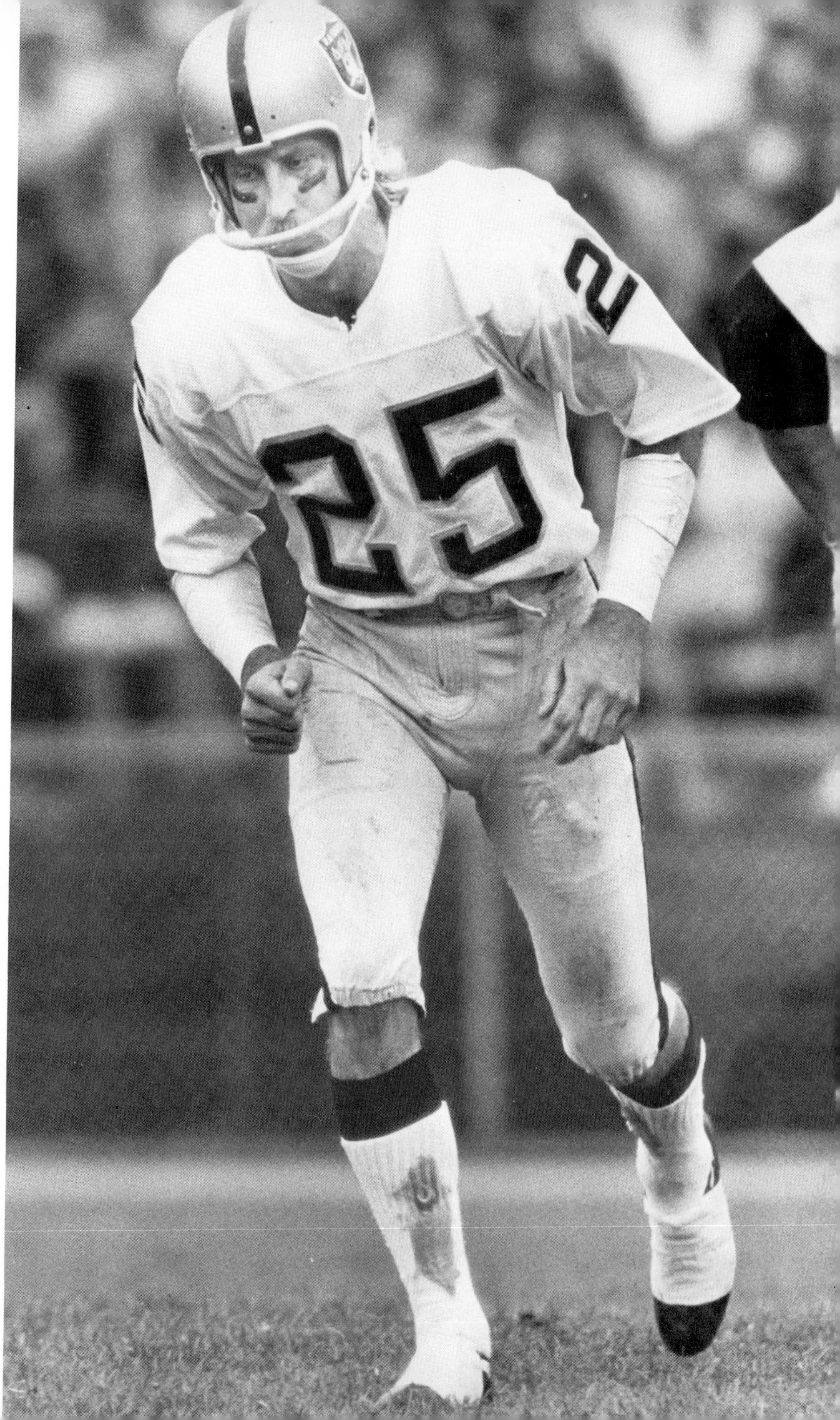

Fred's trouble in holding on to the ball really embarrassed him. If there was one thing he knew how to do perfectly, it was catch a football. He knew he had "good hands."

At Florida State he had caught any kind of pass thrown in his direction. Whether the ball was tossed high or low, short or long, Fred could always haul it in. Whether it came screaming at him like a bullet or floated his way like a hummingbird, he could always grab the football and hold on.

Fred realized what the problem was. In college it had been easy to run pass patterns. But the patterns the pros used were much more complex. The difficulty of the pro system had seriously affected his ability to do what he had always done so well.

"When I go out to catch a pass," he told a friend, "I'm thinking too much about the pattern; I'm not concentrating on the ball, and I drop it."

Fred soon saw that he would have to master the system if he expected to stay with Oakland. Then he began to observe the other receivers at work. They seemed to glide effortlessly through the pass patterns. Almost always they managed to be at the exact spot at the right time. Fred made up his mind that he would learn to do that, too.

But the harder he tried, the more upset he became. The more he studied the playbook, the more confusing and difficult everything seemed.

But he kept on, studying hard and trying to relax. By the end of training camp, he had learned many things. But still the tension he felt continued to interfere with his performance.

Despite his nervousness, Fred was able to do enough right. When the regular season started, he was still with the Raiders. For the first 6 games, he spent most of his

time watching from the bench. Whenever he did get into a game, he was unimpressive. The season figured to be long and frustrating.

Then Fred got his first big break. Oakland had become unhappy with the play of Bo Roberson, one of the regular wide receivers. Then Roberson was traded, forcing the Raiders to use Fred in his place. Oakland's coaches had their doubts about Fred's ability to handle the pressure, but they had no other choice.

In his first game as a regular, Fred surprised them all. He roved confidently over the field, displaying the moves and fakes of a veteran. At last, everything made perfect sense to him. He finished the game with 7 catches for 118 yards.

For the rest of the 1965 season, Fred continued to demonstrate that he was a real pro after all. Although his future now seemed secure, Fred was still unable to relax. Two injuries in 1966 gave him plenty to worry about.

18

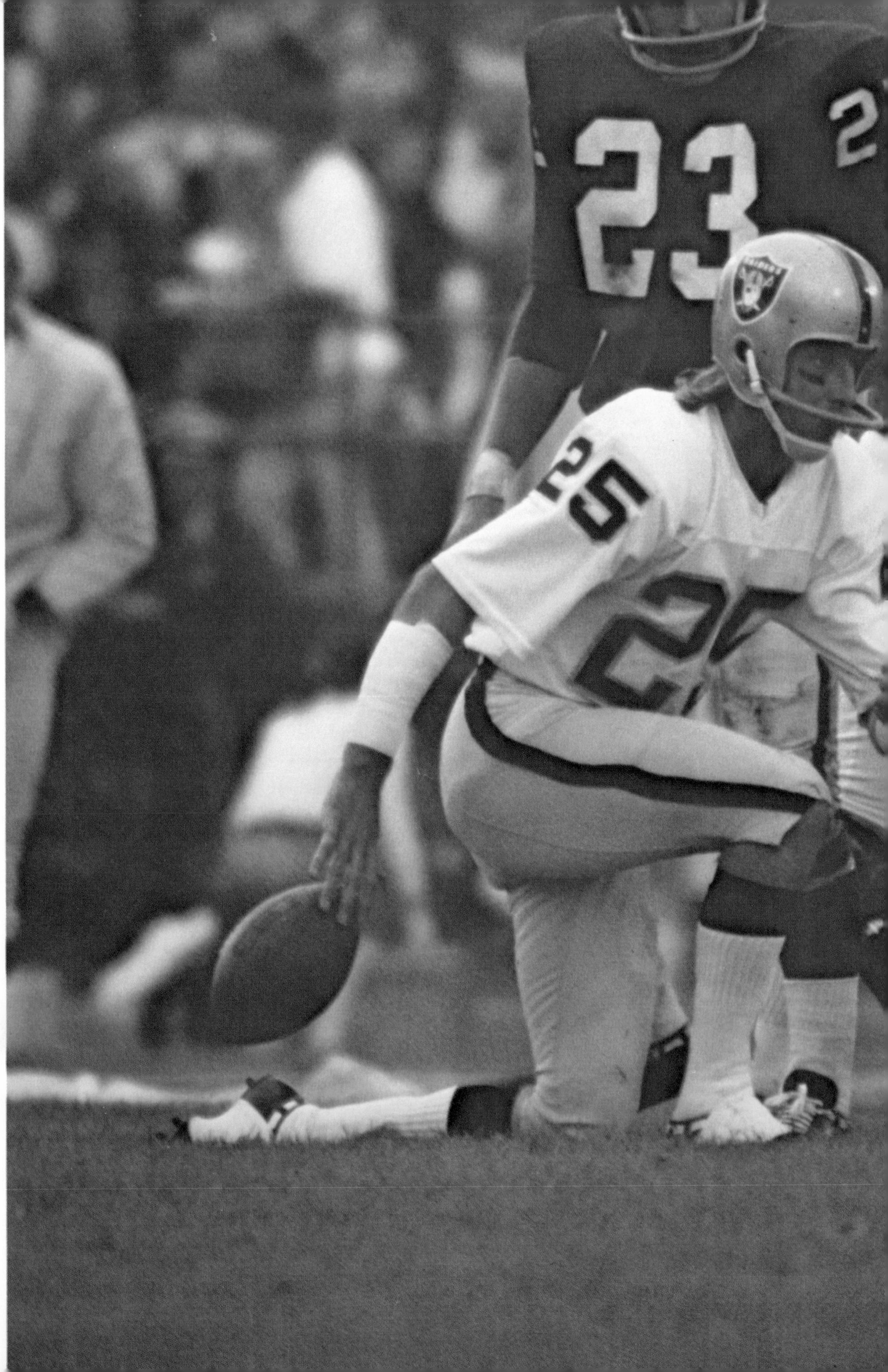

Following knee surgery that winter, Fred reported to training camp in 1967, hoping to get started again. Constant worry about his knee, however, prevented him from performing well at all.

Once again, Fred's chance of making the team looked doubtful. Before an exhibition with the 49ers, he learned that Oakland planned to release 8 players after the game was over. He was sure he would be one of them.

Fred couldn't calm down before the game. But once it started, he had his emotions under control. He was determined to save his job.

On a memorable play in the first quarter, Fred proved how valuable he was to the team. Quarterback George Blanda chose a pass play that called for Fred to slant across the middle. But seeing that the 49er cornerback had figured out the play, Fred faked inside and then cut to the sideline. Blanda

saw what was happening and threw the ball to Fred. Nobody laid a hand on the Oakland receiver as he ran 41 yards for the score.

From there, Fred went on to become one of pro football's most respected receivers. Season after season his reputation continued to grow. It didn't matter any longer that Fred was slow. He made up for it with the surest hands in the pros. He became an expert at running pass patterns.

Perhaps no other receiver in the NFL can match Fred's amazing ability to concentrate. Defensive backs have learned to their disappointment that nothing can upset him on the field.

Fred has often been compared with Raymond Berry, one of the greatest receivers of all time. Like the former Baltimore Colt football genius, Fred never had a great deal of natural talent. But he, too, has worked incredibly long and hard to refine and perfect every move. Today, Fred makes even an impossible catch look easy.

Fred has had many excellent games and seasons in his career. In 1967, his 40 receptions helped pace Oakland to the American Football League (AFL) championship. (At that time in football history, the NFL and the AFL had not yet merged into the 26-team operation known today as the NFL.)

In the AFL championship game the following year, Fred ran for 190 yards on 7 catches. During regular season play in 1968 he caught 61.

Fred had another fine season in 1969, leading the league with 12 touchdown passes. Following further success in 1970, Fred topped all NFL receivers in 1971. His 61 catches accounted for 929 yards and 9 scores. In one game that year he hauled in a spectacular total of 10 passes.

In 1972 Fred led his conference in passing statistics, finishing second overall in the NFL. As a result, he was named to the NFL All-Pro team.

Fred continued to show in 1973 that he was one of the best at his position in the game. At season's end he was picked to play in the Pro Bowl for the fourth consecutive year.

Although Fred Biletnikoff has become a superstar, he is still the same nervous, emotional man he was as a rookie.

Before a game Fred is moody, often complaining about the smallest things. In the locker room after a game, he paces back and forth trying to settle down.

But in between, on the playing field, it is a different story. Even though he may be burning up inside, Fred plays with cool and confident precision. He is too much of a pro to let his emotions interfere with the job he has to do for the Oakland Raiders.

The second half of Super Bowl VIII was about to begin. Miami's Garo Yepremian lined up the ball, preparing to kickoff to the Minnesota Vikings. In the shadow of the goal posts far downfield stood Viking John Gilliam.

As he waited to receive the kickoff, only one thought was in John Gilliam's mind. He would have to do something special now. The Miami Dolphins were leading 17-0, and the Vikings needed a big play. John made up his mind that he'd get it for them.

The crowd roared as Yepremian booted the ball high in the air toward Gilliam. John caught it on the goal line and started to move upfield. He dodged the first wave of hardcharging Dolphins. Then he cut through a second wall of Miami defenders.

Zigzagging across the field, avoiding one tackle after another, John reached the Miami 35-yard line before being brought down. He rose from the turf smiling. His exciting 65-yard return had given the Vikings excellent field position. Perhaps now they could get something started and turn the game around.

But then the expression on John's face changed dramatically. A clipping penalty had been called against the Vikings, wiping out his thrilling run. He watched in disbelief as the officials brought the ball back to deep within Minnesota territory.

From then on, hardly anything seemed to go right for the Vikings. When the game ended, Miami's mighty Dolphins had won their second straight Super Bowl game, 24-7.

John Gilliam

Although his team had lost, John Gilliam had nothing at all to be ashamed about. All season long the Viking wide receiver had come up with big plays.

His efforts had helped Minnesota finish the 1973 regular season with 12 wins and only 2 defeats. No other team in the NFL had a better record; only the Dolphins managed to equal it. John continued to keep up the good work in Minnesota's 2 play-off victories prior to Super Bowl VIII.

John was really spectacular in the sixth game of the season against the Philadelphia Eagles. He caught 6 passes from quarterback Fran Tarkenton for 116 yards and a touchdown. John also threw a touchdown pass himself. On a clever end-around play he passed to another Viking receiver for a 44-yard score. John had made the big difference in Minnesota's narrow 28-21 victory.

In the conference championship game against Dallas, he displayed his skills once again. It was the second half, and the Vikings held a 10-0 lead. After running a pattern up the middle, John suddenly stopped a few yards past the line of scrimmage. Then he turned as if he were about to receive a short pass.

The fake worked, and John dashed by Cowboy defensive back Cornell Green. Catching Fran Tarkenton's pass in full stride, the speedy Minnesota receiver raced 54 yards for the touchdown. After that, Dallas never had a chance. Minnesota went on to win easily, 27-10.

It had been a good year for Gilliam. His 42 pass receptions and 907 yards topped all other Viking receivers. For the second straight year John was chosen to play in the Pro Bowl game.

The Vikings were pleased to have such a fast, versatile wide receiver on the team. John, in only his second year with Minnesota, had given the team the long-pass threat their attack had lacked.

The Vikings' management couldn't help congratulating themselves for making the trade that had brought John from the St. Louis Cardinals to Minnesota in 1972.

The Cardinals were then in desperate need of an experienced quarterback. At about the same time, the Vikings had obtained Fran Tarkenton from the New York Giants. This meant that the Vikings could offer Gary Cuozzo, the team's starter in 1971, to the Cardinals. St. Louis jumped at the chance to get an accomplished passer like Cuozzo. In return, they gave Minnesota Gilliam and 2 future draft choices.

Since then, Cuozzo has retired from football, but John Gilliam keeps rolling along. The Vikings aren't the only ones in the NFL to recognize the importance of the deal. Before Super Bowl VIII, Miami Coach Don Shula told a reporter, "The Gilliam trade has to be one of the all-time great trades."

In his first season at Minnesota in 1972, John sparked the Viking offense with 47 catches for 1,035 yards and 7 touchdowns. His average gain of 23.0 yards per pass led the entire NFL.

John Rally Gilliam was born on August 7, 1945, at Greenwood, South Carolina. At Brewer High School in Greenwood he began to demonstrate an intense desire to win. On many occasions John led his school's football team to victory.

Following high school graduation, John enrolled at South Carolina State College. Even though he played for a small school, his performance on the football field managed to attract the attention of NFL scouts. Then John decided he would give professional football a try after he had graduated from South Carolina State in June, 1967.

After receiving his Bachelor of Science degree in physical education, the 6-foot, 190-pound receiver signed his first NFL contract with the New Orleans Saints.

Like most rookies, he sat on the bench much of his first year. John did see some action, however, and finished the season with 22 catches. In addition to part-time duty as a wide receiver, John ran back punts for the New Orleans team.

In 1968 John continued to learn the many things a pro receiver needs to know. He was still a second-string receiver, but had played enough to gain 284 yards on 24 pass receptions.

The following year found John wearing a St. Louis Cardinal uniform. John was happy about the change and responded impressively. He caught 52 passes that season. His 997 yards and 9 touchdowns established him as one of the top young pass catchers in the league.

John's next 2 seasons with the Cardinals added to his growing reputation. In 1970, he gained 952 yards on 45 catches. John's average gain of 21.2 yards per catch was the highest in the conference. He totaled 42 catches and 837 yards during 1971.

But John Gilliam was growing tired of playing for a losing team like the Cardinals. In his 3 years in St. Louis, the Cardinals had never made the play-offs. So, in 1972, when John heard that he had been traded to the Vikings, he was overjoyed.

Over the years Minnesota had developed a tradition of winning, and John felt certain he could add to that tradition.

He was not mistaken. John has helped the Vikings become one of football's finest teams. But he doesn't intend to stop there. Like all the Vikings, John wants another chance at the Super Bowl.

As he prepared for the 1974 NFL season, John seemed ready to have his very best year ever. He had come a long way since those days on the New Orleans bench. He had learned well and was now rated among the top receivers in running pass patterns. He had the speed, the aggressiveness, and the will to win that every outstanding receiver needs.

John Gilliam felt that 1974 would be the Vikings' year to win it all. And he expected to have plenty to do about it.

Otis Taylor was jumping for joy. It was 1966, and the Kansas City Chiefs had just won the AFL championship.

Otis, in only his second year in the league, had made the difference. "He's our success story," said AFL veteran Fred Arbanas, the Chiefs' tight end. Kansas City Coach Hank Stram was even more lavish in his praise. "Our offense used to go by bus," Stram said. "Now, with Otis, we take the jet."

Hank Stram knew what he was talking about. During the 1966 regular season, Otis had really turned on the speed. He had broken away for touchdowns of 71, 74, 77, and 89 yards. In all, he had caught 58 passes for 1,297 yards and 8 touchdowns that season.

Since then, a truly great season for Otis Taylor has meant an equally fine year for the Kansas City Chiefs.

In 1969 Kansas City was battling the New York Jets for another AFL title. The score was tied 6-6 in the fourth quarter with the Chiefs in possession of the ball on their own 20-yard line. Otis, running a short pattern over the middle, caught the ball and jetted away for a 61-yard gain. He had set up the touchdown that would give the league crown to the Chiefs.

By beating the Jets, Kansas City qualified to play the heavily-favored Minnesota Vikings in Super Bowl IV. In the third quarter, Kansas City led by a slim margin, 9-7. The game was very much in doubt until Otis Taylor made one of the circus catches he is justly famous for.

Otis Taylor

He was running a side-line pattern, designed only to pick up a safe first down. After leaping high in the air to make an over-the-shoulder catch, Otis barrelled over the Viking cornerback who was covering him. Then he saw the field was wide open. Gaining momentum with every stride, he sprinted away for a 46-yard touchdown. The Chiefs now led 16-7, and Minnesota was through for the afternoon. Kansas City later added an insurance touchdown and took the game, 23-7.

In 1970, the Chiefs' first year in the NFL, Otis caught only 34 passes. Kansas City had a mediocre season. But Otis returned to form in 1971, leading the team into the play-offs. Once again, it was apparent that the key to the Chiefs' offense was the ability to get the ball to Otis Taylor. They had gotten the ball to him 57 times, and Otis had rambled for a league-leading 1,110 yards. He was the only NFL receiver that season to top the 1,000-yard mark.

Otis was named to his conference's All-Star team that year. But when it came time to select the All-NFL squad, the Kansas City speedster was overlooked.

Otis was not alone in his disappointment. Coach Stram was really upset. "There's not a better flanker — not a better athlete — in professional football," he said angrily.

Former Dallas Cowboy quarterback Don Meredith agreed. "If ole Otis isn't the best receiver in the league," Meredith remarked in his Texas drawl, "then I don't know who is."

Although Otis was disappointed, he wasn't really surprised. He had never received the acclaim he thought he deserved. "It's the one thing that a player, an individual, sometimes worries about, the lack of recognition," he once told a writer.

Although Otis was highly regarded by NFL coaches

and players, many sports-writers throughout the country had a different opinion of him. He was lazy, they said. They felt that he didn't try hard enough to live up to his potential.

How this rumor got started is hard to say. Perhaps it began because Otis *looks* lazy when he runs. He takes long, loping strides which give the impression that he's not running at full speed.

Kansas City quarterback Len Dawson tried to straighten out the confusion. "Otis has a deceptive way about him," Dawson said. "He'll seem to be gliding along, and then suddenly he'll take off."

The press also thought that Otis had failed to master the technical aspects of the game. They generally rated him below average in running pass patterns.

Once again Len Dawson disagreed with this evaluation of Otis. "What I like about him is that not only has he got fast feet and good hands, he has a good head," Dawson stated. "He sees things out there. He'll come off the field and diagram a pass pattern in the dirt. We've scored on some of those patterns he's drawn in the dirt."

Stung by the criticism that he didn't hustle enough, Otis responded bitterly. "That's the most ridiculous thing I ever heard," he said. "I'll tell you something about Otis Taylor. He wants to be the best — always. There hasn't been a year when he didn't want to score more touchdowns than anybody, gain more yardage than anybody."

Otis had more to say, but he paused to gain control of the anger welling up inside of him. "Every year I start off with the same goals," he continued. "I want to be the number one receiver in the NFL, and I want my team to be in another championship game."

Even if many sports-writers weren't convinced, the NFL's defensive backs knew that what Otis had been saying was true. These men who had to guard him had learned from hard experience.

They knew that he was a constant threat to change the course of a ball game with one exciting gallop down the field. They knew how aggressive he was and how much he wanted to win.

Many cornerbacks had tried to intimidate Otis, but had given up the idea. Former NFL star Johnny Sample once said, "The harder I hit him, the better he seems to play. I found out the best thing to do with Otis is just concentrate on keeping him covered."

Otis had another outstanding year in 1972, making 57 catches for 821 valuable yards. At the end of the season he played the Pro Bowl game for the second straight year. In 1973 Otis

continued to thrill fans everywhere with his intense, exciting style of play.

When he was growing up in Houston, Texas, Otis excelled in all sports. But football was his first love. A star quarterback in high school, he received a scholarship to Prairie View A & M.

At Prairie View, a small, black college near Houston, Otis' coaches decided that he would make a better wide receiver. The move proved beneficial for Otis. He went on to make the small college All-American team.

Then the Kansas City Chiefs heard about him. They discovered that Otis could run the 100-yard dash in 9.6 seconds, Needing a man with this kind of speed, the Chiefs selected him on the fourth round of the 1965 AFL draft. Since then, Otis has been playing the game he loves so well with the energy and fierce determination of a true superstar.

Throughout this pro career, Otis has been a controversial figure in the world of football. Because he always tried so hard to win, his hot temper would occasionally get the better of him. Then a fight would sometimes break out, and Otis would be right in the center of it. Although these fights were rare and never really lasted very long, they received a great deal of publicity. Otis felt the press had exaggerated the incidents. It hurt when kids asked him whether he was mean like the newspapers reported.

"I think I'm a gentle person," Otis once told a sportswriter, "a person who cares about others. For example, I got a call from a lawyer today. A boy I know is doing time in jail. When he gets out, they want someone from the black community who gets along with kids to watch over that boy. I'm going to do it. I want to do it. When people have this kind of faith in me, I don't brush off my responsibility as a citizen."

Otis Taylor had spoken straight from his heart, but he doubted if anybody would really listen.

Years from now when football historians refer to 1972, they might call it the Year of the Perfect Season. It was the year in which the Miami Dolphins sailed undefeated and untied through their 14-game NFL regular season schedule.

Then the Dolphins began to dream of Super Bowl VII. More than anything else they wanted to atone for a humiliating 24-3 loss to the Dallas Cowboys in Super Bowl VI.

But before Miami could return to the Super Bowl, the team first had to get through 2 tough play-off games.

In the play-off opener against the Cleveland Browns, the Dolphins almost didn't make it. With only 7 minutes left in the game, the Browns led 14-13. All day long the inspired Cleveland defense had bottled up Miami's powerful running backs. The Browns had been equally effective in stopping the Dolphins' passing attack.

Double-teamed and sometimes triple-teamed throughout most of the game, Miami's All-Pro wide receiver Paul Warfield had not been able to shake loose. As precious seconds ticked away, Paul realized he had to get something started fast.

It made him shudder to think that Miami's perfect record would be shattered. Everything he and his teammates had worked so hard all year long to accomplish would mean nothing if Cleveland held on to win.

The Dolphins had the ball on their own 20-yard line, far away from the Cleveland goal line. Proud and confident, Paul shouted encouragement to his teammates in the huddle.

Paul Warfield

Dolphin quarterback Bob Griese faded back to pass. He looked upfield for Paul, firing the ball to the swift receiver for a first down at the Miami 35. The Dolphins were on their way.

A few plays later, Paul made one of the breath-taking pressure catches that have become his trademark in the NFL. The Browns' line was rushing hard as Griese threw the ball toward Paul deep in Cleveland territory. The pass was overthrown, but Paul jumped high in the air, juggled the ball for a split second, and then held on. With a Cleveland defender on his back, Paul crashed hard to the ground on the Browns' 20-yard line.

Griese called for another pass to Warfield 2 plays later. Paul darted gracefully toward the sideline, faking with his head and his feet. Frustrated by Paul's acrobatics, Cleveland linebacker Bill Andrews gave him a shove. Interference was immediately called, moving the ball to the 8-yard line.

From there, Griese played it safe and handed off to his running backs. When Jim Kiick finally went over for the touchdown, Miami had escaped defeat. Victory was sweet for Paul Warfield. He had made the big plays just when they had counted the most.

Miami continued its march to greatness a week later, beating the Pittsburgh Steelers. Then the Dolphins extended their winning streak to 17, with a Super Bowl VII victory over the Washington Redskins.

The following year, the Miami team won Super Bowl VIII. This time the Dolphins' victim was the Minnesota Vikings. These 2 Super Bowl triumphs convinced many football experts that the Dolphins were the greatest team ever to play the game.

Miami's achievement had come as the result of the combined efforts of a whole cast of superstars. Still, there could be no doubt that Paul Warfield had played a major role in the team's amazing success.

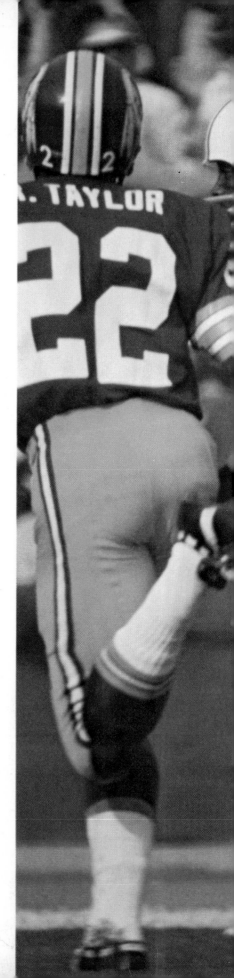

44   A brilliant all-round receiver, Paul seems to have no weaknesses. His mere presence on the field poses a constant threat to even the finest defensive team.

Dallas Cowboy Coach Tom Landry, a thoughtful judge of football talent, has high praise for Paul. "Warfield," Landry said recently, "is the premier receiver in the business." Most NFL coaches and players agree that Paul is truly in a class by himself. He has been selected All-Pro 7 times in his 10-year career.

All NFL teams know that there is no way to stop Paul completely. But they know they can limit his effectiveness somewhat by using 2 defenders to cover him. For this reason, Bob Griese does not throw the ball to Paul very often.

Naturally, Paul would like to catch more passes. But he has learned to wait patiently for his chance. When it comes, he manages to make the most of it.

Although he has never led the NFL in total receptions in any season, Paul has caught the big ones for long yardage. In 1970 he had only 28 catches, ranking low on the list of top receivers. But an average gain of over 25 yards per reception led his conference. In 1973 he totalled 29 catches, but 11 of them went for touchdowns.

Paul's value to the Dolphins cannot be measured solely by the important catches he makes or the touchdowns he scores. Another indication of his greatness is the damage he can do when he *doesn't* have the ball.

Paul is a superb decoy. He can often fool the defense into thinking that the ball will be thrown to him. Drawing defenders away from the real play, Paul gives the other Dolphin receivers an opportunity to get free.

Paul's football career began in high school in Warren, Ohio. By the time he

graduated, he had received 45
over 70 scholarship offers
from colleges all over the
country. He chose Ohio
State.

In addition to being a star
halfback in football, Paul
was the leading member of
the track squad. One of the
best long jumpers in the na-
tion, he was considered a
good bet to make the 1964
U.S. Olympic team.

Paul wanted to go to the
Olympics. He also wanted to
play pro football in 1964 for
the Cleveland Browns, who
had drafted him. It was a
difficult decision to make.
But Paul realized that football was to be his career, and
he was eager to get started.

In his rookie season with
the Browns, Paul caught 52
passes for 9 touchdowns. At
season's end he was chosen
to play in the Pro Bowl game.
For the next 5 seasons at
Cleveland, Paul was one of
the NFL's brightest stars.

Paul was happy in Cleve-
land. He had bought a home
there for his wife and 3 chil-
dren. The Browns were a

46 solid ball club, always in contention for the NFL title. Everything seemed perfect. Then one night Paul received bad news. Cleveland had traded him to the Miami Dolphins for the 1970 season.

The Dolphins had won only 3 games in 1969. It wouldn't be easy playing for a poor team after all the years of glory in Cleveland. It wouldn't be easy, either, to leave his home. But Paul took the news calmly, "I just had to convince myself to be optimistic," he later told a reporter.

Then he heard that Don Shula had become the Dolphins' new coach. Paul was aware of the great success Shula had achieved as the coach of the Baltimore Colts. Now there was reason to hope. Things were beginning to look better already.

The rest is history. In 1970 Miami made the playoffs and have been almost unstoppable ever since. And Paul long ago realized what a lucky break that trade had been for him.

They call Paul Warfield "Mr. Unemotional." Just as he controls any game he appears in, he also controls his emotions. Paul is not afraid to express his opinions and feelings or to listen to those of others. But if anyone starts to argue with him, he simply refuses to continue the conversation.

"I'm a loner," Paul once said. "I'm not one you can get close to. But I'm human."

Miami fullback Larry Csonka has expressed his admiration for the player and the man. "Paul Warfield is one of the all-time great receivers," Csonka said. "He is also one of the all-time great guys."

The 1974 season will be Paul's last in the NFL. He has agreed to play in the new World Football League (WFL) in 1975. Paul's 3-year WFL contract will pay him over a million dollars. Most fans who have seen Paul's grace and daring on the football field feel he's worth every penny of it.

stars
of the
NFL

The Running Backs
The Receivers
The Linebackers
The Defensive Linemen
The Coaches
The Quarterbacks

CREATIVE EDUCATION